THE GREAT OUTDOORS! #@%&*!

Cartoons by John Troy

Nick Lyons Books

"Ha Ha, fooled you!"

"May I suggest the rainbow trout. They're really quite fresh."

"You're *always* hot."

"I'll be damned glad when hunting season is over."

"In that case there's really no point in us trying it."

"Of course I heard you say, 'Toucan live as cheaply as one,' I just didn't think it was funny."

"Well I'll be darned, look what's caught on my sleeve."

"Hello, Snug-As-A-Bug-In-A-Rug sleeping bag company?!!"

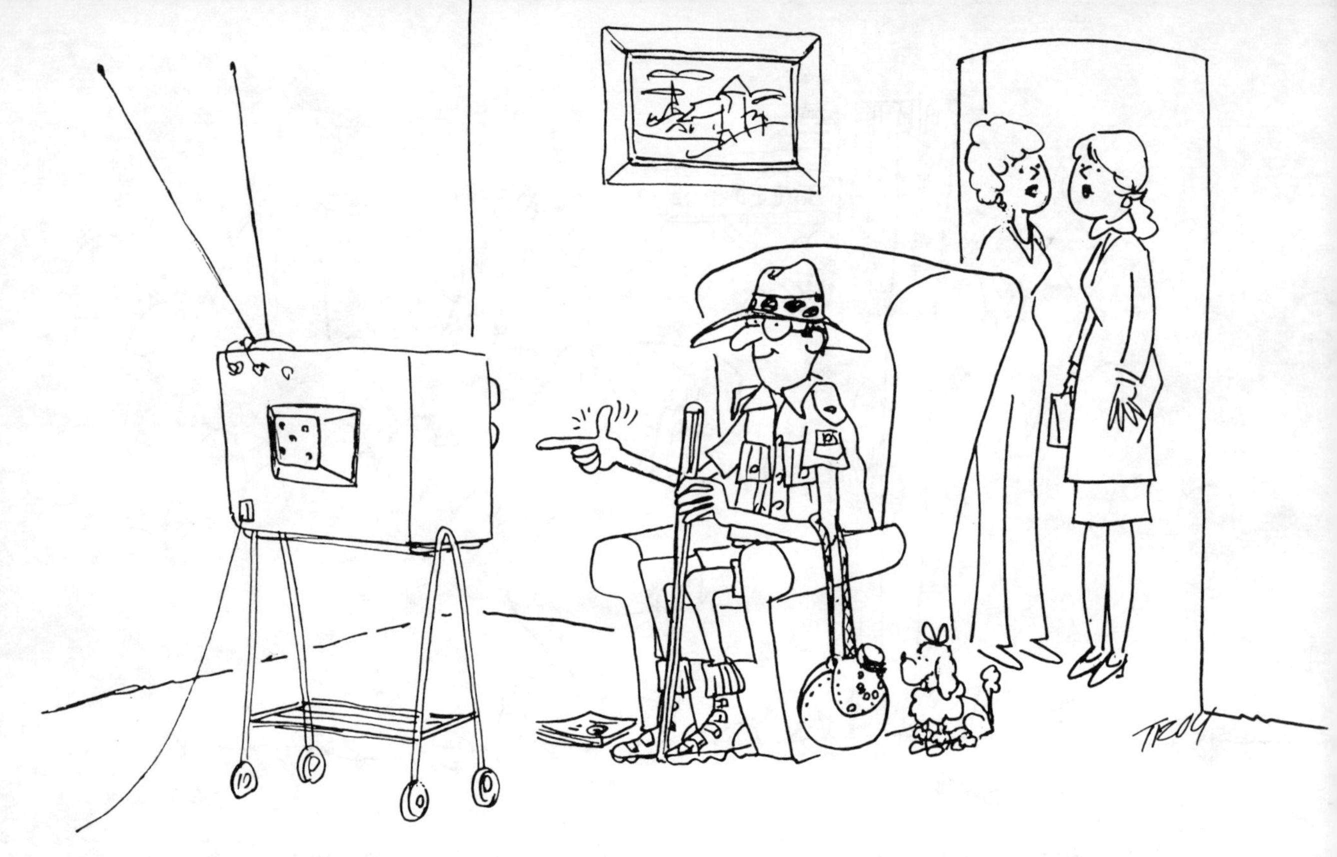

"PBS is Edmond's only link to the great outdoors."

"Great, now what country are we going to ski across?"

"Is that the way you get your kicks, by watching us spawn?!"

". . . and this is the last slide from that particular trip."

"He says he's got some good news and some bad news. First the bad news—we're lost. But now the good news—we're making very good time!"

"It's Darwin's only chance to practice when he's in the city."

"You'll have to do something about your squirrel chasing dogs in the park. It doesn't look right."

"Well, so much for lambs being easy prey for us eagles."

"I love white-water rafting, but frankly I'd like to spend more time in the raft."

"Guess who made some new friends while we were out hunting?"

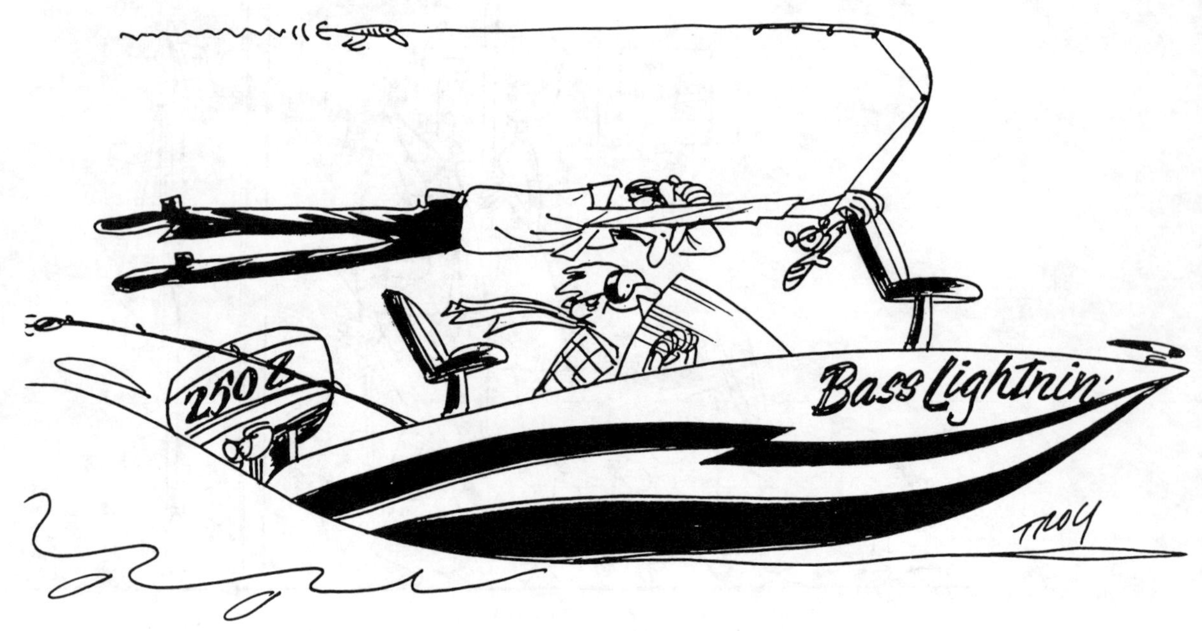

"Is this WARP ONE or WARP TWO?"

"No, no, not cacoon hat, *racoon hat. R-A-c-o-o-n!*"

"So, I'm the first salmon you've ever hooked on a fly, eh?"

"Sure, the canoe cuts the wind for him!"

"If it weren't for your steering we'd never make it through these rapids!"

"Make the first shot count!"

"Play dead, it's our only chance."

"He said this is the first time he's ever been confused for more than a week."

"I am very honored to be your guest speaker . . . "

"At Safari Unlimited the safety of our clients is uppermost in our minds."

"YOU tell him he can't be our leader."

"What a pleasant surprise, a gyrfalcon *and* a canvasback duck!"

"We have a complaint. They say with a name like 'Dodo' they don't stand a snowball's chance in You-know-where."

"Some people are just muggable."

"... Excuse me." "Whoops. My fault." "Sorry! You first."
"Pardon me." "S'cuse me." "Look out!" "Pardon. . ."

"Stop badgering me!"

"I picked up this habit at a cancer research center."

"This is your last chance—either the dog goes or I do!"

"Serves you right."

"Spot, go find a safe place to sit."

"When does squirrel season open?"

TROY

"I understand you've been training snakes."

"To you it's *lunch*, to me it's *bait*!"

"Your father is a real turkey."

"Toxic waste . . . acid rains . . . nuclear seepage—my word, Ellen, do you think the world is going to *disintegrate*?"

"Hmm, down . . . down? Now that's a very good question."

"Good Heavens, George, don't resist—give him the peanuts!"

WIPE YOUR FEET BEFORE ENTERING
TROY

"I view Harold as renewable matter slowly dissolving into fuel, rather than a man in the October of his years."

"STOP HOUNDING ME!"

"Look at that hatch!"

"They get pushy every time Autumn arrives."

"What, remove him and ruin a perfectly good story!"

"See if I take *you* hunting again!"

"Sweetheart, the mice have gotten into your apple pie."

"All I know is he jumps out of a tree and runs with me every morning."

"How long have you been hunting these toxic dump sites?"

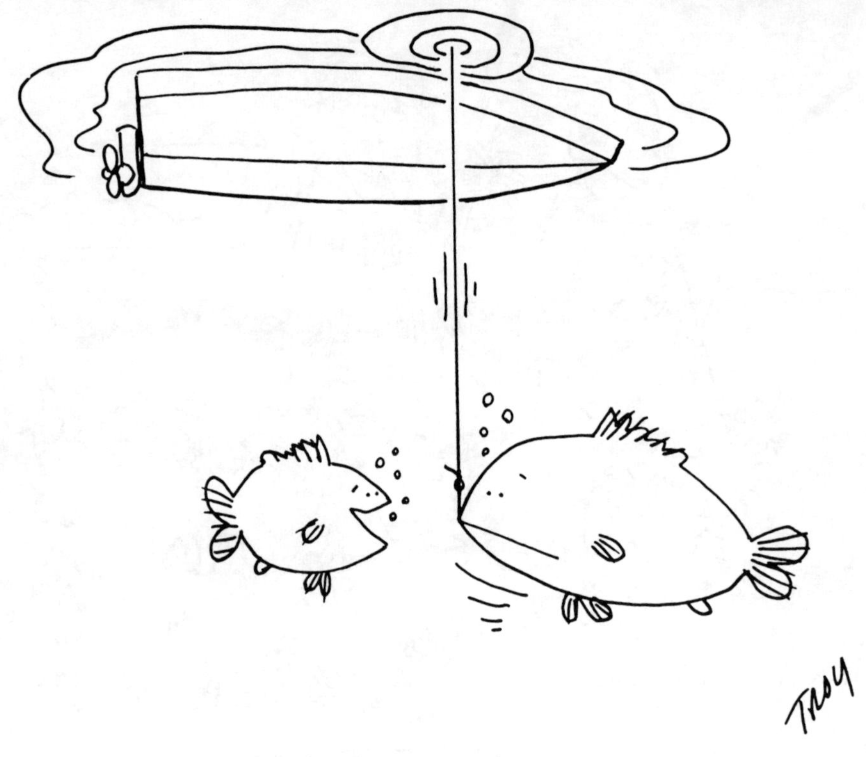

"This might not be a good time to ask, Pop . . ."

"Worms, grub, shiners . . . nope, no ants."

"It was such a damned good shot I couldn't resist having it mounted."

"Kiss 'Mister Selectivity' goodbye."

TROY

SALMON
RIVER
THE
END
IS
NEAR!

"Boy, these salmon put on quite a show, don't they!"

"I said a *Heimlich* hug!"

"Around here, pinpoint casting is a must."

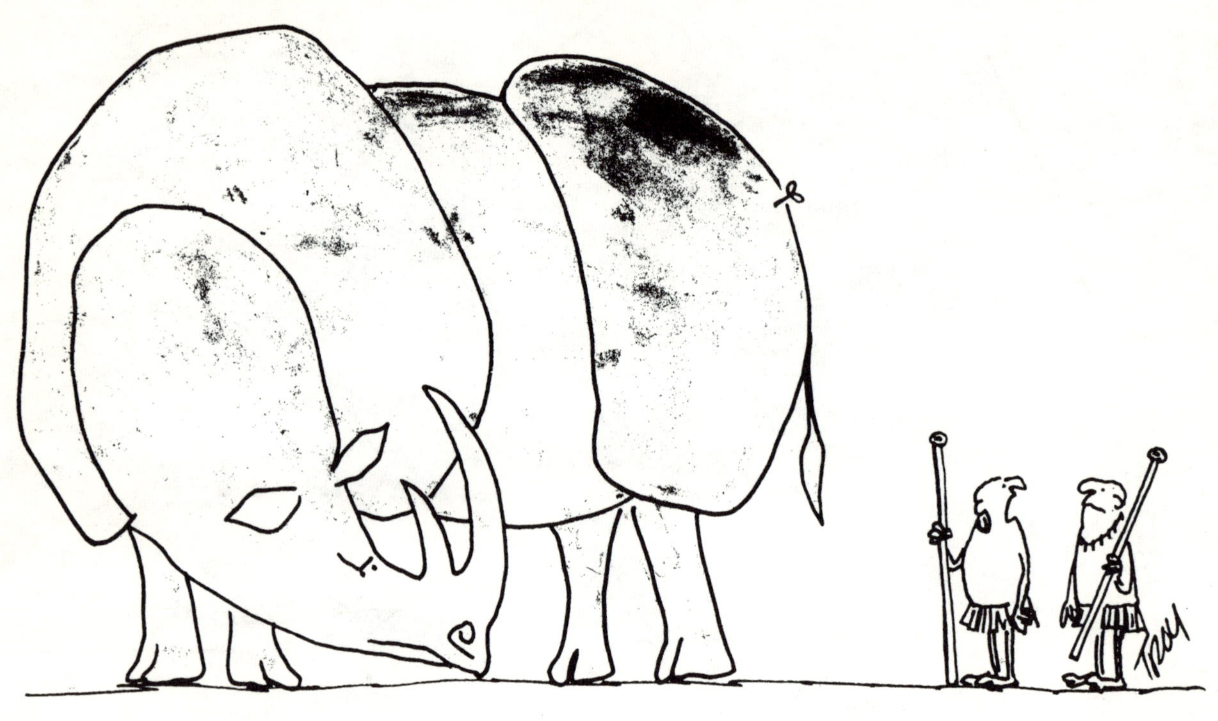

"Tell me you didn't say, 'I forgot to dip the dart in curare'."